Rewire Your Anxious Brain

How to calm states of anxiety with simple exercises

Dr Lowelle Ramsson

Copyright © 2021 Dr Lowelle Ramsson

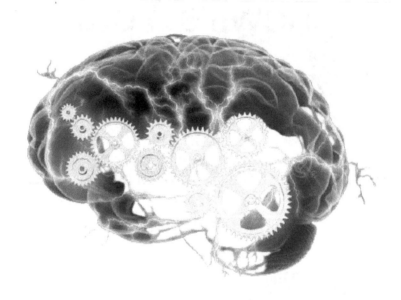

Table of content

Why do you have the symptomatism of "feeling restless, throbbing and alone" ?

Symptoms such as "feeling restless" and "pounding and loneliness" are called "anxiety" and "tension" and are a type of emotion that everyone experiences.

It's a normal reaction to have these symptoms when you have something to worry or care about, when meeting a superior or someone you're meeting for the first time, or before an exam, and it's not an illness. The symptoms naturally go away when there are no worries causing them.

The problem is when symptoms such as "restlessness" and "pounding and loneliness" occur without such a reason.

In this case, it may be "morbid anxiety".

Unlike "normal anxiety," "morbid anxiety" has the characteristics that it occurs for no reason, is out of proportion to it, and continues forever even if the cause disappears. While "normal anxiety" has the necessary aspects for humans, such as preparing for danger and becoming the driving force to act towards problem solving, "morbid anxiety" is a mental or physical illness and can be a symptom.

If you experience any of the above symptoms and suspect that it is "morbid anxiety," have them diagnosed by a psychiatrist or psychosomatic physician.

Before that, it is a good idea to have a general idea of what anxiety is and what kind of illness it is.

Anxiety is defined psychiatrically as "an unfocused feeling of fear." A similar word is "fear," but it is used for "when there is an object" (sometimes not distinct).

Anxiety is accompanied by physical symptoms, one of which is "pounding" (palpitations), but there are also "chest tightness," "breath distress," "cold sweat," "trembling," and "fluttering." symptoms such as "dizziness," "numbness of limbs," "weakness," "frequent urination," "thirst," "insomnia," and "headaches" appear.

These are primarily due to the work of the autonomic nerves, particularly the sympathetic nerves.

This is because emotions and autonomic nerve functions such as sympathetic and parasympathetic nerves are closely related in the brain.

There are many types of anxiety.

Acute, sudden anxiety is called panic (or panic attack if repeated) (also called an anxiety attack).

Symptoms of anxiety typically observed in "panic disorder", suddenly hit by severe anxiety for no reason, heartbeat (palpitations), rapid pulse (tachycardia), chest constriction, choking, dizziness, etc. at the same time, and I think I might die at any time.

However, it will naturally disappear over time.

When seizures recur, there is anxiety that "I can come back" (called anticipatory anxiety), so when a seizure occurs, I am afraid of places and situations where I cannot escape or get help. It is accompanied by the symptomatism of " agoraphobia."

This is a type of anxiety disorder called a "phobia."

Other phobias include "social phobia (abnormally tense in public and fear of embarrassment)" and "specific phobia (elevation, claustrophobia, animals, darkness, etc.), Fear)."

Unlike panic attacks, there is also a type of anxiety symptom in which less intense anxiety persists chronically, called generalized anxiety.

Generalized anxiety is typically observed in the case of generalized anxiety disorder.

In addition, obsessive-compulsive disorder and posttraumatic stress disorder are also mental illnesses that belong to anxiety disorders and each has its own characteristic anxiety symptoms.

Refer to each explanation page for details.

Anxiety disorders are a group of mental illnesses whose main symptom is anxiety, and panic disorder is a typical example. In addition to the above, some anxiety disorders are caused by general physical illnesses and substances. There are also diseases.

General physical diseases that cause it are endocrine diseases such as hyperthyroidism and hypoglycemia, heart failure, pulmonary embolism, arrhythmia, cardiovascular/respiratory diseases such as chronic obstructive pulmonary disease (COPD) and vestibular dysfunction.., Nervous system diseases such as encephalitis, causative substances are intoxication from caffeine, stimulants and other illegal drugs, withdrawal symptoms that occur when alcohol or medically administered sedatives, sleeping pills, anti-anxiety medications, etc. are suddenly discontinued.

Although these are mental symptoms that appear to be anxiety, the cause is due to physical illness or substances, so it is important that they are properly examined and diagnosed.

In some cases, it is directly life-threatening.

When you see your doctor, be sure to report that you were taking the medication.

There are many other mental illnesses that come with anxiety symptoms besides anxiety disorders.

It is safe to say that there is no mental illness without anxiety symptoms.

In depression and schizophrenia, anxiety can be the main symptom.Depression often presents with frustration, anxiety, guilt, and hopelessness mixed with depressive symptoms.

Schizophrenia experiences disturbing and severe anxiety associated with distinctive psychotic symptoms such as delusional mood, paranoia, and hallucinations.

In addition, hypochondria (somatic symptom disorder) causes excessive anxiety about the body and illness.

In "adjustment disorder," which is a stress response, anxiety symptoms are the most common symptoms along with depressive symptoms.

Another anxiety disorder peculiar to children is "separation anxiety disorder," which indicates severe anxiety about being separated from parents and attached people.

There are various treatment methods

Treatments for depression vary from person to person.

If you have typical depression, you can expect the effects of drug therapy. If the personality and environment have a strong influence, a psychotherapeutic approach and sometimes the environment needs to be improved. If the cause is another illness or drug, you should consider treating the illness or changing the drug. Regarding leave of absence, there are cases where it is necessary to take leave and there are cases where it is better to continue working, and there is no single policy in this respect as well.

It is important to know that there are many different types of depression and there is more than one cure, rather than being treated as one with depression. Your depression is different from the depression of others, and it is natural that each person has a different treatment.

Signs / symptoms of depression

How long has it lasted?

A good way to diagnose depression is that some of the following symptoms last for more than two weeks: Each symptom feels like everyone feels, but if it feels almost constant all day long and lasts for a long time, it may be a sign of depression.

Depressed mood (depressed, heavy mood)
No matter what I do, it's not fun, I'm not interested in anything
I'm tired but can't sleep, sleep all day, wake up much earlier than usual
I'm frustrated and I feel like I'm being urged by something
Feel like you've done something wrong and blame yourself, feel worthless
Thinking is weakened
Want to die

There are also signs that you can see from the surroundings

In depression, there are not only changes in the mood that

you feel, but also changes that you can see from your surroundings. If people around you notice such a change that is "unusual," you may be suffering from depression.

The expression is dark

Tears became brittle

Slow reaction

Restless

DUI increases

There is also a sign that appears on the body

Changes may appear in the body before the depression is noticed.

Have no appetite

Feel heavy body

Get tired easily

No libido

Headache and stiff shoulders

Palpitations

Stomach discomfort

Tend to constipation

dizzy

Thirsty

This is just a guide.

Is it strange? Does that apply? If you think so, first consult an expert. There are specialists in psychiatry and psychosomatic medicine at general hospitals, or psychiatric clinics, but if you don't know where to go, you can consult with your doctor who knows you well, or you can go to your hometown. Let's use the consultation counter of the public health center or mental health and welfare center.

Collecting one-sided information on the Internet or in books and making a self-diagnosis is not recommended because it only delays the chance of receiving correct medical treatment.

The diagnostic criteria for depression that are used these days are very easy to understand, and it seems that you can easily diagnose whether you have depression. However, it is difficult to make an accurate diagnosis of whether you are really depressed or what type of depression you have without a proper judgment by a specialist.

Treatment for depression

Various treatment methods
If the cause of depression is clear, it may be considered to eliminate it.

For example, if the cause is a physical illness, it is treated, if the effect of the drug is suspected, the drug is stopped if possible, and if that is not possible, the drug is changed to another drug. A psychotherapeutic approach is effective for those who are personally susceptible to stress. Even with such depression, if the depression is severe, treatment with antidepressants is also performed in parallel.

If depression is determined, treatment with antidepressants is generally given. However, even with typical depression, if the condition is mild, the effect of the drug may not be so high, so drug therapy is not absolute. Check with your doctor to see if you really need the medicine before getting treatment.

There are various medicines

There are several groups of antidepressants, from SSRIs (selective serotonin reuptake inhibitors) and SNRIs (serotonin-noradrenaline reuptake inhibitors) to tricyclic antidepressants. In addition, antidepressants and sleep-inducing agents are also used according to the symptoms. In addition, people who have experienced mania or hypomania are diagnosed with mania (bipolar disorder) instead of depression, and mood stabilizers are used. Which medicine works depends on the person receiving the treatment, and even for the same person, it depends on the stage of the disease.

How to take medicine

In drug treatment, first ask your doctor to explain the effects and side effects of the prescribed drug. It is also important to adhere to the prescribed amount and frequency. If you feel that the symptoms are not so severe, or if you are worried about side effects, if you reduce the amount or frequency by yourself, your doctor will decide that the effect will not be sufficient and increase the amount of the drug, or another drug. You will have to think about measures such as changing to.

If you have any concerns about side effects, don't judge by yourself, but talk to your doctor to find a solution. This kind of approach to the attending physician also leads to the development of a relationship of trust.

Talk to your doctor if you have any concerns or doubts about treatment

If you have any concerns or worries about proceeding with treatment, talk to your doctor. Having a relationship with your doctor who can talk to you about anything is the first step in treating depression.

If your doctor doesn't answer your treatment concerns or questions, or if you find it awkward to talk to you, consider listening to other specialists. This is called a second opinion.

Hearing the opinions of multiple specialists can be a way to get convincing medical care.

Depressed mood, depressed state, depression

Symptoms such as "depressed" and "depressed" are called depressed moods. Depressed state is a state of strong depressed mood. The term depression is more commonly used in daily life, but it seems that psychiatry often uses the term depression. When this kind of depression is more severe than a certain level, it is called depression.

Classification of depression

Here are some typical methods for classifying depression. It may be divided into extrinsic or somatic, intrinsic, psychogenic or personality environmental factors in terms of cause. Somatic depression is when a brain disorder such as Alzheimer's disease, a physical disorder such as hypothyroidism, or a drug such as adrenocortical steroids causes depression.

Intrinsic depression is a typical type of depression, and antidepressants usually work well and are said to improve over a period of time without treatment. However, it goes without saying that it is better to treat the patient as soon as possible, considering the suffering of the person and the risk of suicide.

If you have a manic state, it is called bipolar disorder.

Psychogenic depression is when personality and the

environment are strongly associated with depression. Depressive neuropathy (neurotic depression) is sometimes called, and when the environmental influence is strong, it is also called reactive depression.

Recently, classification from a different perspective from the depression classification that emphasizes such causes is often used. For example, the American Psychiatric Association's diagnostic criteria for DSM-IV has an item called "mood disorder," which is divided into depressive disorder and bipolar disorder. In addition, depressive disorders include major depressive disorders with certain symptom characteristics and severity, and less severe but long-lasting dysthymia.

The above two classification methods are classifications from different standpoints, and each has its own strengths and weaknesses. Some people sometimes misunderstand that "intrinsic depression = major depressive disorder" and "depressive neurosis = dysthymia", but it is important to use them properly.

Cause / Factor of onset

The typical type of depression is intrinsic depression, as mentioned above. Depressive episodes are called depressive episodes because they are said to be depressed for a certain period of time and improve without treatment. Depressive episodes may recur after healing.

Depressive episodes can be triggered by environmental stress, but they can also occur without causing anything. It is speculated that neurotransmitters in the brain, such as serotonin and noradrenaline, are impaired in these types of depression. However, this is also considered because drugs that act on serotonin and noradrenaline may be effective in depression, and it has not been fully proven yet.

It should be considered that it is not yet clear whether serotonin or noradrenaline is involved in depression with possible causes, such as physical depression and personality-environmental depression described at the beginning. Let's do it.

For example, one of the known drugs that cause depression is interferon (IFN). It is said that the cause of depression caused by IFN is related to the action of IFN, which is slightly transferred from the blood into the brain, the action via the adrenal cortex and thyroid gland, and the action related to dopamine and interleukin. It's complicated.

On the other hand, in a depressed state such as being relatively healthy on holidays, the influence of personality is often large, and the influence of neurotransmitters does not seem to be so large. In such cases, the advice that "depression is not that your heart is weak or indulgent, and that serotonin, noradrenaline, etc. are not working well, so you should take medicine and take a rest" is the opposite. It may be effective.

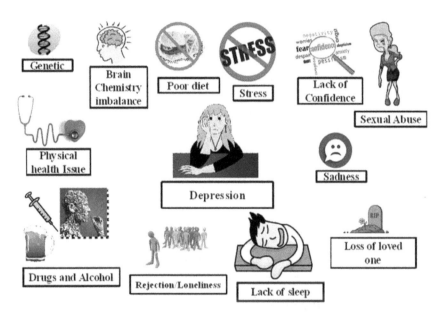

Symptoms

Table 1 shows the common symptoms of depression. It is also important for early detection. If you notice a change in your physical or mental condition that is different from your usual self, or if you are around you, and if you notice a different person's appearance, think of depression at least once.

Table 2 shows the diagnostic criteria for major depressive episodes of DSM-IV. Quite strict criteria (such as not being met unless depression is fairly severe), such as "almost all day, almost every day," "in all, or almost all activities," and "existing in the same two weeks." Please note.

Table 1 Symptomatology in depression

1) Symptoms that you feel
Depressed, feeling heavy, depressed, sad, anxious,
frustrated, lack of energy, lack of concentration, do not want to do
what you like, worry about details, bad Feel like you've done something and blame yourself
, think things bad, want to die, can't sleep

2) Symptomatology seen from the surroundings
Dark facial expression, fragile tears, slow reaction,

restlessness, increased drinking

3) Symptoms of the body

Loss of appetite, tiredness, tiredness, lack of libido, headache, stiff shoulders,

palpitation, stomach discomfort, constipation, dizziness, thirst

Table 2 Diagnostic Criteria for Major Depressive Episodes (DSM-IV)

Major Depressive Episode

A   Five (or more) of the following symptoms are present during the same two weeks, causing changes in premorbid function. At least one of these symptoms is (1) depressed mood or (2) loss of interest or joy.

Note: Obviously, it does not include general physical illness or symptoms of delusions or hallucinations that do not match mood.

Depressive mood almost all day, almost every day, as indicated by the person's own statement (eg, feeling sadness or emptiness) or the observation of others (eg, appearing to shed tears).

Note: Children and adolescents can feel frustrated.

Significant diminished interest and joy in all or almost all activities, almost all day, almost every day (as indicated by one's statement or observation of others).

Significant weight loss or weight gain (eg, a change of 5% or more of body weight in a month), or almost daily loss or gain of appetite without a diet.

Note: Also consider that for children, the expected weight gain is not seen.

Almost daily insomnia or excessive sleep.

Almost daily psychomotor agitation or arrest (observable by others, not just a restless or cursed subjective sensation).

Almost daily fatigue or diminished energy.

Almost daily sense of worthlessness, or excessive or inappropriate guilt (sometimes delusional, not just guilty of blaming yourself or getting sick).

Poor thinking and concentration, or difficulty making decisions is observed almost daily (either by one's own statement or by others).

Repetitive thoughts about death (not just the fear of death), repetitive suicidal ideation, suicide attempts, or explicit plans to commit suicide without any special plans.

B   Symptoms do not meet the criteria for mixed episodes.

D   Symptoms are not due to the direct physiological effects of the substance (eg, substance of abuse, medication) or general physical illness (eg, hypothyroidism).

E   Symptoms are not well explained by bereavement

reactions. That is, after losing a loved one, the symptoms last for more than 2 months, or there is significant dysfunction, morbidity to worthlessness, suicidal ideation, psychotic symptoms, psychomotor deterrence. It is characterized by that.

Treatment

The usual way of thinking about depression treatment

Awareness-raising activities such as "depression is a cold in the heart. Let's take medicine and take a rest as soon as possible" may be spreading in an inappropriate manner. I feel that the number of patients who are trying to cure with drugs has increased, disregarding the mental problems that must be considered, and that the number of doctors who have no choice but to change the type of drug to be given has increased. Here are the main ideas for treating depression.

Consider whether a physical illness or drug is the cause of or affects depression. If possible, consider treatment of physical illness or discontinuation or change of medication. Again, if the depression is severe, antidepressant therapy is also used.

If your depression is not related to your physical illness or medication and your depression meets the criteria shown in Table 2, consider antidepressant therapy. However, there are reports that antidepressants are not very effective when depression is mild, so the expected efficacy and side effects of antidepressants should be carefully considered. In addition, in the depressed state of manic-depressive disorder, as a general rule, antidepressants are not used, and drugs classified as mood stabilizers are prescribed.

If the environmental stress is high, consider whether it can be adjusted and deal with it. If you are a depressed person who has not been able to adapt well in various situations in the past and you have a personality problem to consider, you should consider it together as a psychotherapy.

Antidepressant therapy

Recently, so-called SSRIs (serotonin reuptake inhibitors) are often used when antidepressant therapy seems to be preferable.

SSRIs are often thought to have few side effects, but headaches, diarrhea, and nausea are common. In addition, when you start taking the drug, you may have serotonin syndrome, and when you lose or stop taking the drug, you may have a withdrawal syndrome, which may make you feel more anxious and irritated.

You may hear stories like "SSRIs have made it possible for non-psychiatric doctors to treat depression," but it's not that easy to use. Although the drug treatment policy may be indicated by the classification of SSRI or SNRI (serotonin noradrenaline reuptake inhibitor), the difference in side effects and drug interactions between drugs is not small. For each drug, you should read the treatises and package inserts and use them appropriately. First of all, it is important to take it exactly as prescribed.

Other treatments

Psychotherapy for depression includes cognitive behavioral therapy and interpersonal therapy. As one of the cognitive-behavioral therapies, rework aimed at returning to work is attracting attention, even if it takes time to verify its effectiveness. Convulsive electroconvulsive therapy for the elderly, who are prone to intractable depression and the side effects of antidepressants, is also an important option.

Progress

It is not easy to describe the general course of depression in an era when the range of depression is widespread and people think of "depression" differently.

Depression, which is greatly affected by physical illness and drugs, is the key to cure of the physical illness and whether the drug can be reduced or changed.
Depression diagnosed as "intrinsic depression" or "major depressive disorder without other psychiatric disorders" is often treated with antidepressants and is cured at a high rate. However, antidepressant therapy and psychotherapy to prevent recurrence need to be adequate. On the other hand, if you are diagnosed with "depressive neurosis" or "dysthymia", it depends on how much you can adjust the

environment and how much you can think about how to deal with your personality and situation with your doctor. Outcomes vary greatly.

If you are diagnosed with major depressive disorder and are accompanied by disorders such as anxiety disorder, somatic symptom disorder, and personality disorder, treatment is generally more complicated and improved than with major depressive disorder alone. Is often delayed.

Advice to patients

Even if you say depression, how you feel and how your family responds will differ greatly depending on what type of depression you have.

The most important thing is to have a reliable doctor. It is most important to get the advice that suits you from your doctor.

And no matter what type of depression you have, there will always be days when you feel better, no matter how long it takes, so never think about suicide.

It is difficult to give advice that applies to the treatment of all people with depression, but for example, with typical depression, it is difficult to fall asleep, while waking up early in the morning and even feeling in the morning. For those who are very bad, even the advice "Let's try to live a regular life early to bed and early rising" can be a word that can be distressing or pushing. It is said that when you are depressed, it is better to take medicine and take a rest, but it is better to think that this also applies to some depressions.

Research status

The concept of depression may have become more ambiguous as the scope of depression has expanded. Depression research continues to be extensively studied in terms of biology and psychotherapy.

The first is the development of new antidepressants. Drugs with few side effects and strong effects have been released little by little.

Research that seeks to elucidate depression biologically includes molecular biological research, neuroendocrine research, research using animal models, and imaging research. In particular, near-infrared spectroscopy is attracting attention as being useful in diagnosing depression.

On the psychotherapy side, there are many reports on cognitive-behavioral therapy, return-to-work programs, depression in children, and their relationship to suicide.

"Seasonal Depression" Depressing in Winter 5 Ways to Strengthen Your Mental

"I feel more depressed," "I feel depressed," and "I feel tired and tired easily." Does anyone feel that way? If so, "seasonal depression" is suspected, with increasing incidence from autumn to winter.

"Winter blue" whose onset increases in winter

Among depressions, there is "seasonal depression" in which symptoms appear every year from autumn to winter. The disease is also referred to as "seasonal affective disorder" (SAD).

Seasonal depression is characterized by periodicity. Every year, the symptom begins to appear from October to November when the daylight hours are short, and recovers around March when the sunshine is long. From that symptomatology, there is another name, "winter blue" (winter depression).

Seasonal depression is a serious illness that can interfere with daily life if the symptoms are severe.

Main Symptoms of Seasonal Depression

□ Often depressed □ I
can't handle the work I was able to do before

□ I'm tired and tired easily, I'm tired of moving my body

□ I can't enjoy what I've enjoyed so far

□ My ability to think and concentrate is clearly weakened □ I sleep longer than usual, I can't get up in the morning

□ My appetite is reduced or increased, and I eat too much, mainly carbohydrates.

Why the onset increases from autumn to winter

The reason why seasonal depression is more likely to occur during the fall and winter seasons is that the amount of protein called "serotonin transporter" (SERT) in the brain fluctuates significantly as the daylight hours decrease. ..

A research team at the University of Copenhagen in Denmark conducted a test called positron emission tomography (PET) in patients with seasonal depression and healthy people to see what changes are occurring in their brains.

The results showed that people with signs of depression, especially those with winter onset, had 5% higher SERT levels than those with summer onset.

SERT regulates neurotransmission by recovering the neurotransmitter "serotonin" in the brain. Elevated SERT levels and deficient serotonin levels contribute to depression.

Due to the disturbance of the "body clock"

Another cause of seasonal depression is the disturbance of the "body clock." A research team at RIKEN Brain Science Institute investigated why the body clock is likely to be disturbed in winter.

The human body has a function to adjust the body clock called "circadian clock", which regulates sleep and wakefulness and the rhythm of hormone secretion. A nerve called the "suprachiasmatic nucleus" in the hypothalamus of the brain controls the circadian clock throughout the body and acts like an orchestra conductor.

For example, jet lag, shift work, and irregular life can cause you to feel unwell or feel unwell because the suprachiasmatic nucleus does not work well. When it becomes dark in autumn or winter and the circadian clock cannot synchronize with the light and darkness of the sun, the physiological function is affected.

The research group found that there are two areas for adjusting the circadian clock, which repel each other in the summer and increase the deviation in synchronization, and attract and decrease in the winter. The suprachiasmatic nucleus is said to read not only the daily cycle but also the one-year cycle.

It improves when it is actively exposed to the morning light

A regular lifestyle, where you wake up in the morning and soak up the sun, is effective in preventing and treating seasonal depression. From autumn, when the sun starts to get shorter, you should take advantage of walking and commuting time to actively take in the morning light.

When exposed to sunlight during the day, a substance called serotonin is produced. Serotonin is a source of melatonin, a sleep hormone secreted by the brain. During the winter months when the sun is low, serotonin is reduced and melatonin is not sufficiently produced.

Melatonin has the effect of adjusting the circadian clock, such as seasonal rhythm, sleep / wake rhythm, and hormone secretion rhythm, and its deficiency makes it more likely to cause modulation.

5 ways to relieve seasonal depression

1 Eat a nutritionally balanced diet

A deficiency of serotonin causes disorders in the functioning of the brain. It is important to get enough nutrients such as proteins, vitamins and minerals necessary for serotonin production in the diet. Proteins such as meat, fish, and soybeans contain "tryptophan," which is one of the essential amino acids required for the production of serotonin, so it is recommended to take it in just proportion.

2 Exercise such as walking

You may not want to move as much as possible in the cold season, but habituation of exercise has a great effect on your mind and body.

By vigorous exercise, one of the neurotransmitters that control feelings, "dopamine," is secreted, which has the effect of improving symptoms when feeling depressed or suffering from frustration.

Just walking fast in the sunlight makes a big difference. By exercising, you can feel refreshed and active. Starting exercise is the first step in improving your lifestyle.

3 Find someone who can speak your feelings

If you have seasonal depression and are suffering alone, your depression will increase. So let's talk to someone about that feeling.

If you don't have someone close to you to talk about your feelings, find a support group and talk about your feelings there. You should be able to feel refreshed by going out and meeting people as much as possible.

In addition to direct "social participation," you can also get in touch with nature and history, have hobbies such as finding hidden stores in the area, and chat with someone.

4 Brighten your home / work place

All that is needed to improve seasonal depression is more exposure to natural light. However, the days are shorter in winter, so it's hard to do so. If possible, it is effective to replace the lighting in your home or workplace with a brighter one.

"High-intensity phototherapy" is often used for treatment. It is a treatment method that adjusts the biological clock and adjusts the biological rhythm by being exposed to sunlight or equivalent light, and is said to be effective in many patients.

5 Create and organize a "ToDo list"

A pile of things to do can make you feel uncomfortable, but a well-organized and well-organized task or project can alleviate depression and depression.

Create a to-do list, prioritize what you can do, and develop a productivity style that suits you, clarifying your goals and tasks. It's full of untouched tasks, freeing you from headaches. If you can move smoothly from task to task, you may be less depressed.

_____
_____
_____
_____
_____
_____
_____
_____
_____
_____
_____
_____
_____
_____

Dissociative disorder

Dissociative disorder is a condition in which you lose the sense of yourself. For example, there are various symptoms such as the memory of an event is completely lost, the feeling of being in a capsule is unrealistic, and the person is in a place that he or she does not know.

Under these circumstances, the one in which multiple personalities appear in oneself is called multiple personality disorder (dissociative identity disorder). When one personality appears, there is often no memory of another personality, which causes various problems in life.

These symptoms are thought to be a type of defensive reaction that occurs in an attempt to separate the painful experience from oneself. In treatment, it is very important to create a safe environment and for family members and others to understand the illness.

Dissociative Identity Disorder Symptoms

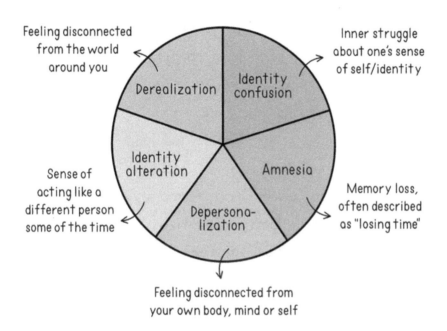

Feeling disconnected from the world around you

Inner struggle about one's sense of self/identity

Sense of acting like a different person some of the time

Memory loss, often described as "losing time"

Feeling disconnected from your own body, mind or self

Derealization

Identity confusion

Identity alteration

Amnesia

Depersona-lization

What is dissociative disorder?

Our memory, consciousness, perception and identity (ego identity) are essentially united. Dissociation is a condition in which the ability to organize these sensations is temporarily lost. For example, some of your past memories may be lost, you may not feel part of your perception, or your emotions may be paralyzed. However, in the dissociated state, new perceptions and behaviors that are not normally experienced may appear. Abnormal behavior (running and others) and the formation of new personalities (multiple personality disorder, shamanism, etc.) are typical examples. These dissociation phenomena, if light and temporary, can also occur in healthy people.

A condition in which these symptoms are serious and interfere with daily life is called dissociative disorder. The cause is said to be related to stress and trauma. There are many types of this trauma. Some are transient, such as disasters, accidents, and assaults, while others are chronically repeated, including sexual abuse, long-term confinement, and combat experiences.

In order to avoid the damage caused by such a painful experience, it is thought that dissociative disorder is caused by the mental suspension of some functions as an emergency evacuation.

Symptoms of dissociative disorder

Dissociative disorders have a variety of symptoms. The World Health Organization Diagnostic Guideline ICD-10 lists the following categories of dissociative disorders:

Dissociative amnesia: A mental stress that causes the memory of an event to be lost. Many will regain their memory within a few days, but sometimes it can be long-term.

Dissociative tongue: Symptoms such as loss of the sense of who you are (identity), disappearance and starting a new life. They are often exposed to extreme stress at school and at work, and suddenly begin without being able to reveal it to anyone, often losing their memory of themselves.

Catalepsy: The body becomes stiff and immobile.

Dissociative stupor: The inability to move or exchange words.

Depersonalization: The feeling of being yourself is impaired and you feel as if you are looking at yourself from the outside.

Dissociative epilepsy: Psychological factors that cause symptoms such as coma, immobility, and loss of sensation.

In addition, hysterical ataxia, hysterical deafness, dissociative dyskinesia, incontinence, psychogenic deafness, psychogenic tremor, dissociative spasm, wrath spasm, dissociative sensory disorder, psychogenic hearing loss , Nervous eye fatigue, Gunther syndrome, subacute confusion, acute mental confusion, psychogenic deafness, psychogenic confusion, multiple personality disorder, reactive confusion, non-alcoholic subacute confusion, etc. It is a kind of.

Multiple personality disorder: Of these, multiple personality disorder is named dissociative identity disorder by DSM (American Psychiatric Association Diagnostic Guidelines) and exhibits extremely characteristic symptoms. Patients have multiple personalities, and those personalities take turns. Personalities often do not remember each other while another personality is appearing, which often interferes with their lives.

These dissociative symptoms are often difficult to understand and believe in. You may be suspected of being malingering, especially if the illness gain is involved. There are also cases where it is difficult for even a specialist to make the diagnosis.

An important point in understanding dissociative disorders is that in the past they have been of interest in psychiatry in many ways without the term dissociation. There is a series of psychiatric disorders called culture-bound syndrome (a psychiatric disorder specific to a particular culture), but almost all of those listed there can be considered dissociative disorders.

Treatment of dissociative disorders

Basics of treatment

The basis of treatment for dissociative disorders is to create a safe treatment environment, understand the people around you, such as your family, and have a relationship of trust with your doctor. The main cause of dissociative disorders is the inability to express oneself to others due to mental stress. In other words, the dissociated part of the mind can only be expressed in a reassuring relationship.

Many of the symptoms of dissociative disorders usually resolve spontaneously or shift to another after some time. Eliminating dissociative amnesia, aphonia, aphonia, paralysis, etc. by hypnosis or suggestion at an early stage is not only ineffective, but may worsen the symptoms. It is also important to have an attitude of watching the natural course of these symptoms while providing a safe environment and opportunities for self-expression.

About psychoeducation and information provision

It is important that the therapist has a good knowledge of dissociative disorders in general and is proactive in providing information to patients and their families. Most patients with dissociative disorders have the problem of being distrustful of their condition and appearing to be acting, which can exacerbate their dissociative symptoms. Also, there are many cases where the person does not understand what is happening to him / her. The first step in adjusting the environment is for the person and his / her family to understand the disorder and accept the symptoms.

Drug therapy

It is said that there is no effective drug for dissociative disorders. Antipsychotics do not seem to be very effective for hallucinations, which are often confused with schizophrenia. Rather, medications are prescribed for comorbidities that exacerbate the symptoms of dissociative disorders. For example, antidepressants for depressive symptoms and tranquilizers for neurotic symptoms, including PTSD.

Eating disorders

Eating disorders include anorexia nervosa, which causes you to eat very little, and bulimia nervosa, which eats extremely large amounts. Anorexia nervosa has symptoms such as reduced food intake, extreme weight loss due to eating only low-calorie foods, and loss of menstruation. Bulimia nervosa has symptoms such as being unable to stop once you start eating, eating and vomiting, regretting eating too much, and becoming depressed. Anorexia nervosa can lead to bulimia nervosa.

He has a strong desire to lose weight, so he does not want to be treated. However, undernutrition can lead to various physical disorders and even death, so it is necessary to convey the importance of treatment. Eating disorders are often caused by various stresses, and the understanding and support of those around us is very important.

What is an "eating disorder"?

Do you have morbid anorexia nervosa or overeating?

Abnormal eating behavior can be broadly divided into "anorexia nervosa", which does not want to eat, and "overeating", which eats an extremely large amount of food.

A little bit of anorexia nervosa or overeating is something that many people experience. It seems that many people have experienced a broken heart, losing their appetite, or eating too much to relieve stress. However, these abnormal eating behaviors become excessive, and even if you lose weight extremely, you cannot stop eating, and you try to avoid weight gain by spitting out everything you ate after overeating or using laxatives and diuretics. When the act of doing is seen, this raises the suspicion of anorexia nervosa requiring treatment.

The trauma behind anorexia nervosa and overeating

These extreme feeding behavior abnormalities appear in the background of the extreme commitment to weight, "I don't want to get fat, I want to lose weight," and the belief that "I'm fat and ugly → I'm not worth it." There is a psychological background such as. In addition, especially for young women, the social value that "being thin is beautiful" also has an effect. In addition, the experience that parents had a bad relationship with each other when they were children and that their parents and other people around them told them that their weight and body shape were not good also contributed to eating disorders.

Anorexia nervosa in teens and bulimia nervosa in 20s

Many people develop anorexia nervosa in their teens, and bulimia nervosa tends to occur in their twenties. Both types are 90% female. However, it has been pointed out that the number of male eating disorders has increased recently. Anorexia nervosa and binge eating seem to be the opposite symptoms, but they often change from binge eating to binge eating and from binge eating to binge eating.

It's a serious illness that can be life-threatening.

Eating disorders are not as simple as a diet failure, and if left unchecked, they can lead to physical and mental illness and tiredness, which can lead to death. Especially in the case of anorexia nervosa, if you lose weight to 60% or less of your normal weight, you are more likely to have serious complications such as renal failure due to undernutrition, hypoglycemia, arrhythmia due to electrolyte abnormalities, and infections such as tuberculosis. In addition, both types are prone to complications of mental illness such as alcohol and drug dependence, depression, anger, and personality disorder, and are impulsive such as shoplifting, sexually unrestrained, self-harm, and suicide. There will be more action.

Signs / Symptomatology of Eating Disorders

Is it anorexia nervosa?
If you think, let's look at the weight first

Is it anorexia nervosa? If you think so, let's look at your
weight first. (Enter numbers in half-width characters)
1. How tall are you?
cm

2. If you are this height
 kg is the standard weight.

3. What is your weight?
kg

4. This weight is the standard weight
 It becomes%.

Less than 80% of normal weight is too thin. If you continue
to weigh this much for months, it may be one of the
symptoms of anorexia nervosa. A healthy lean person is
unlikely to fall below 80% of normal weight.
Do you have menstruation?
Anorexia nervosa is considered if you weigh less than 80%

of your normal weight and have no menstruation.

If you have these symptoms, you may have bulimia.

Weight is close to normal weight and is neither obese nor thin.

I can't stop eating a lot in a short time when there are no family members or no people such as midnight.

Especially when you feel stress, you want to overeat.

I'm happy that I don't have to think about anything when I'm eating, but after eating, I fall into a fierce self-loathing.

I'm worried about eating too much and getting fat, so I put my finger in my throat and vomit, and try to excrete it by force using laxatives and diuretics.

Treatment of eating disorders

In the case of an eating disorder, the patient is extremely afraid of gaining weight due to the treatment, so it is difficult to be convinced of the treatment.

It is important for schools, family and friends to work together with specialists to support them so that they can continue treatment properly.

Also, in the case of teenage patients, the relationship with their parents and other family members often affects their illness, so it is necessary for the family members to receive counseling regarding how to treat patients and the family environment. Will be. Choose a hospital that has an eating disorder specialist or counselor for treatment. Inpatient treatment is also provided if weight loss is extreme or if the family environment is not suitable for treatment.

Treatment is centered on psychotherapy to normalize weight commitment and incorrect self-evaluation, and drug treatment and nutritional guidance are provided as needed with the aim of recovering the mind and body.

Panic disorder / anxiety disorder

Panic disorder is a condition in which you suddenly have seizures such as palpitation, dizziness, sweating, choking sensation, nausea, and tremors in your limbs, which interfere with your life.

This panic attack is so strong that I think I'm going to die and I feel I can't control it myself. As a result, you become anxious about what to do if you have another seizure, and avoid places and situations where seizures are likely to occur. Especially in a closed space such as in a train or elevator, you may feel that you cannot escape and you may not be able to go out.

In panic disorder, psychotherapy is given to gradually get used to what you are not good at, in addition to treatment with medicine. It is important not to overdo it and work at your own pace. Let's watch the surroundings slowly.

What is "panic disorder / anxiety disorder"?

If you are suffering from unexplained death-like pain that is difficult for others to understand

Suddenly my chest became painful and my heartbeat was just "beating the bell". Cold sweat makes my back full.

"Maybe I'll die ..." I was taken to the hospital by ambulance while being attacked by such anxiety, but no matter where I looked, my body was normal, and in the meantime, the painful symptoms disappeared. Even though I'm anxious about repeating such seizures over and over again, no one understands. Those who came to this page may have experienced such thoughts.

Panic is a reaction that is prepared to survive the danger of death

Many people panic when faced with a sudden life threat, such as a fire or earthquake. My heart beats faster, I feel bloody, I can't think about things calmly, and I feel like I want to scream out loud. You may also vomit something in your stomach. You may not be able to stay still and start running blindly. All of these reactions are beneficial for your escape from enemies and disasters, and are your body's survival program.

However, some people may react like a panic when nothing happens. Even though there is no danger of life, you will feel anxiety and fear as if it were life-threatening, and you will experience symptoms that you can see in a panic state on your body. This is called a panic attack.

Never die from a panic attack

Even if it is said that there is nothing wrong with it, if you have many life-threatening seizures, you will be worried that you may die from this seizure. But you won't die from a bout of panic disorder.

I'm not a wolf boy

Panic disorder basically involves repeated panic attacks. Family members, friends, and people at work who were initially worried will gradually start to make a fuss when they find out that there is nothing wrong with them. It's like a wolf boy's story. It's painful that no one understands it, even though it's really painful, painful, and anxious.

1 in 100?

Panic disorder is by no means a rare illness. It is said that one or two out of every 100 people will have a panic disorder in their lifetime. For example, at least one or two people in a Shinkansen regular car may experience a panic disorder. Recently, there have been reports that more people have panic disorder.

It is also said that it is more likely to occur in women than in men.

Signs / symptoms of panic disorder / anxiety disorder

Do you have panic attacks, anticipatory anxiety, or agoraphobia?

Panic disorder begins with a panic attack. At first, there are only panic attacks, but as the attacks are repeated, symptoms such as anticipatory anxiety and agoraphobia begin to appear when there are no seizures. It may also be accompanied by depressive symptoms.

Panic Attack

Do you have

repeated unexpected panic attacks ? Repeated "unexpected panic attacks" are a characteristic symptom of panic disorder. An "unexpected seizure" is a seizure that occurs regardless of the situation. Therefore, seizures may occur while sleeping.

Panic attacks can be seen without panic disorder. For example, a person with claustrophobia may have a panic attack when confined in a small space. However, this is a reaction that occurs when faced with a particular situation, not the "unexpected seizure" seen in panic disorder.

Anticipatory anxiety

Do you always feel anxiety that you may have another

seizure ? As you repeat panic attacks, you become afraid of the next seizure even when you have no seizures. Anxiety such as "I think I'll have another seizure", "I think I'll have a more severe seizure next time", "I'm going to die this time", and "I'll be crazy when the next seizure occurs" will disappear. This is "anticipatory anxiety," a common symptom of panic disorder.

Another symptom of panic disorder is that behavioral changes such as quitting work occur due to anxiety about when a seizure will occur.

Agoraphobia

I feel like I'm going to have a seizure when I go there. Is there a place I'm not good at? When a

seizure occurs, I'm ashamed that I can't escape from it or I can't get help. You will have a place that you are not good at, and you will avoid that place or situation. This is called "agoraphobia". The place I'm not good at is not always the square. There are various places where people feel scared, such as going out alone, getting on a train, or going to a hair dressing shop. In addition to agoraphobia, there are also fears of going out and fear of space.

Agoraphobia makes you unable to work or do your daily life,

and tends to withdraw, which affects your relationships with your friends. Since I can't go out alone, I feel more sorry for myself, who depends on others. There are some panic disorders that are not accompanied by agoraphobia, but in most cases agoraphobia is present.

How to treat panic disorder

For the treatment of panic disorder
Treatment with medicine
Psychotherapeutic approach there is.

Treatment with medicine

Purpose of treatment

The primary goal of drug treatment is to "prevent panic attacks," followed by "reducing anticipatory anxiety and agoraphobia as much as possible."

Commonly used medicine

Generally, the first drugs used are SSRIs and other antidepressants and benzodiazepines, a type of anxiolytic.

Quantity and number of times

Since the effects of these drugs vary from person to person, it is necessary to increase or decrease or change the drug while checking the effects. To check the effect correctly, take the medicine in the amount and number of times specified by your doctor.

Panic disorder is a disorder in which drug therapy is effective. It is not a good idea to "cure only with feelings without relying on medicine".

Talk to your doctor if you have any concerns or doubts

If you have any concerns or doubts about taking your medication or treatment in general, don't hesitate to talk to your doctor to resolve it.

Psychotherapeutic approach

In panic disorder, it is important to use psychotherapy in addition to drug treatment. In particular, cognitive-behavioral therapy has been shown to be as effective in treating panic disorder as drug treatment.

When the medicine starts to work and the seizures do not occur, it is part of the treatment to gradually challenge going out, which was not good.

However, it is forbidden to overdo it, so please consult with your doctor or counselor and work on it with the intention of slowly moving forward step by step.

Sleeping disorder

Sleep is very important for your health. Sleep helps to relieve physical and mental fatigue, and also has the role of establishing memory and strengthening immune function. Maintaining a healthy sleep leads to a vibrant daily life.

People tend to think of insomnia when it comes to sleep disorders, but it has become clear that many people have sleep problems due to various illnesses other than insomnia. When night sleep is impaired, symptoms such as drowsiness, drowsiness, and poor concentration also appear during the day. It can be said that sleep problems and daytime problems have a front-to-back relationship. If you have these sleep problems or daytime sleepiness problems for more than a month, you may have some kind of sleep disorder. Treatment of sleep disorders depends on the cause. Knowing your sleep status and sleep problems is important for getting proper treatment.

What is a sleep disorder?

Sleep disorder is a general term for various illnesses

A sleep disorder is a condition in which you have some sleep problems. Sleeplessness is common, but sleeplessness is not equal to insomnia. There are various causes of insomnia, including those caused by the environment and lifestyle, those caused by mental and physical illness, and those caused by drugs.

In addition, sleep disorders include not only insomnia, but also many illnesses such as being sleepy during the day, morbid exercises and behaviors that occur during sleep, and sleep rhythms that are disturbed and irreversible. I will. In addition, sleep problems are often caused not only by one cause or illness, but also by a combination of several factors.

Multifaceted examination and organization of what is wrong with sleep, what is the cause, subjective symptoms and objective information will lead to appropriate diagnosis and treatment.

What's wrong with sleep disorders?

What's wrong with sleep disorders? For one thing, sleep disorders can interfere with daily and social life. When sleep disorders cause daytime sleepiness, drowsiness, and poor concentration, they interfere with daily life and, in extreme cases, can lead to accidents.

In addition, if sleep deprivation or sleep disorders persist for a long period of time, you may be more likely to develop lifestyle-related diseases and depression. For these reasons, it is important to properly deal with sleep disorders.

Signs / Symptomatology

Signs and symptoms of sleep disorders can be broadly divided into 1) insomnia, 2) excessive daytime sleepiness, 3) abnormal behavior and abnormal perception / abnormal movement that occur during sleep, and 4) problems with sleep / wake rhythm. It can be summarized in one. There are also symptoms such as snoring and drowsiness that are pointed out by people around you.

Understand the signs and symptoms from both the ones that you are having trouble with and the ones that people point out, and ask a specialist to make a proper judgment about the suspected illness.

Symptomatology that can be noticed

Insomnia (bad sleep, unable to fall asleep again due to waking up in the middle, waking up early in the morning, unable to sleep soundly) → Check for mental illness, physical illness, medications, and the following sleep disorders, and then determine whether or not you have insomnia.

Hypersomnia (I can't help but sleep during the day, I take a nap and be careful) → Check for sleep deprivation and illnesses that deteriorate the quality of sleep. Examine hypersomnia Dysesthesia at bedtime (I can't sleep well because my legs are itchy or burning, or I can't keep my legs still, and it gets worse after the evening) → Check for restless legs syndrome Problems with sleep / wake rhythm (I can't fall asleep at the appropriate time and can't wake up at the desired time) → Check the sleep / wake rhythm in the sleep diary Check the circadian rhythm sleep disorder

Symptoms pointed out by people

Snoring / Apnea (Snoring, holding your breath when you are asleep, suddenly choking as if you were snoring) → Check your weight, drinking, and medications Check for sleep apnea syndrome Abnormal behavior during sleep (sleeping behavior, somniloquy, loud / screaming during sleep) → Check the relationship with dreams, whether to wake up and wake up, check for parasomnia Abnormal movements during sleep (legs are moving jerks at night or when falling asleep) → Check for abnormal sensations at bedtime Investigate periodic limb movement disorders.

About sleep hygiene

Check your sleep hygiene as well as your symptoms. Poor sleeping environments and incorrect sleeping habits may interfere with sleep.

Bedroom environment (noise, sunlight, brightness when sleeping, TV and radio)

Sleep habits (time to go to bed, time to get out of bed, time to actually fall asleep, time to actually wake up, habitual sleep, nap) Luxury items (drinking, smoking, caffeine such as coffee)

About treatment

Treatment of sleep disorders depends on the disease. It is not "sleepless" equal to "hypnotic treatment". It is important that the underlying disease is properly diagnosed from the symptoms, signs, medical examinations and tests, and that treatment is given according to the cause.

Treatment for diseases other than insomnia
Sleep apnea syndrome
Treatment depends on the severity. Nasal continuous positive airway pressure (nasal CPAP therapy) and oral devices are used. If you are obese, you need a diet. Drinking and sleeping pills make it worse.

Restless legs syndrome / periodic limb movement disorder
Antiepileptic drugs and antiparkinsonian drugs are used. You need to see a specialist.

Hypersomnia

Get enough sleep at night and try to live a regular life. Take a short nap well, such as during your lunch break. Central nervous system stimulants may be used for drowsiness, but require medical attention and examination by a specialist.

Parasomnia

Stress may be involved, so try to reduce stress. Prepare a bedroom environment that takes risks into consideration when you fall asleep during sleep. Hypnotics, antiepileptic drugs, antidepressants, antiparkinsonian drugs, etc. are used as drug therapy.

Circadian rhythm sleep disorder

To reset your body clock and keep up with the normal rhythm of the day, get plenty of light in the morning. The trick is to get up at the same time even on holidays and get in the light. Seek the guidance of a specialist when using sleeping pills or supplements.

Hypnotic treatment

Sleeping pills are used for insomnia symptoms such as difficulty falling asleep, getting up halfway, and waking up early. Antidepressants, anxiolytics, and antipsychotics may also be used. Follow the usage and dosage prescribed by your doctor and use it correctly. Never take sleeping pills with alcohol. Get to bed within 30 minutes of taking sleeping pills.

If you stop taking sleeping pills all at once, rebound may worsen your insomnia. Stop slowly under the direction of your doctor.

Review of sleep habits

I don't care about sleep time

The older you get, the less sleep you need. Do not aim to sleep for too long, but set a sleep time that suits your age.

Get to the floor after getting sleepy, don't be too particular about bedtime

When I am enthusiastic about sleeping, my head becomes clearer. If you stay on the floor without falling asleep, you will become anxious and impatient about not being able to sleep, and you will become even more unable to sleep.

Wake up every day at the same time

Wake up at the same time every day, no matter how many

hours you slept.

Do not spend on the floor for purposes other than sleeping

Avoid watching TV or reading on the floor. If you have trouble sleeping, get off the floor and do your own relaxing thing.

Take a short nap, at the latest before 15:00

Long naps and naps after the evening adversely affect sleep at night.

7 Types of Relaxation Techniques That Help You Fight Stress!

1. Practise Deep Breathing

Are you distracted? Try deep breathing. A simple yet powerful relaxation technique, deep breathing involves taking slow, long, deep breaths. And as you do so, you focus on disengaging your mind from distracting sensations and thoughts. This type of breathing exercise is particularly helpful for people with eating disorders and sleep disorders, as it helps them to focus on their bodies in a more positive way. Deep breathing exercises may help activate the parasympathetic nervous system, which controls your body's relaxation response. There are many types of deep breathing exercises, like abdominal breathing, diaphragmatic breathing, and paced respiration. These exercises can be combined with other de-stress activities, like music and aromatherapy. The best part – it is easy to learn and can be practiced anywhere.

2. Progressive Muscle Relaxation

This is a two-way process, where you systematically contract and relax different muscle groups in the body. Practising PMR (Progressive Muscle Relaxation) regularly makes you familiar with what complete relaxation feels like. This enables you to react to the initial symptoms of muscular tension accompanying stress. And as your body relaxes, so does the mind.

3. Body Scan Meditation

Do you often ignore the signs your body exhibits due to stress without realizing the seriousness of the situation? This could lead to serious health issues in the near future. Body scan meditation is a great way to release tension that you might not even realize your body is experiencing. The technique involves paying attention to different body parts and bodily sensations in a gradual sequence starting from the toe and then moving up to the head.

4. Guided Imagery

Did you know your stress levels could go down just by drawing a scenic picture in your head? Well, that's exactly what 'guided imagery' does to you. For this particular relaxation technique, you imagine scenic locations and pictures in your mind to help you focus and relax. You will find plenty of recordings of soothing scenes online on free apps – all you need to do is choose the image you find calming, one that has a personal significance.

5. Mindfulness Meditation

This type of relaxation technique involves sitting in a comfortable position, focusing on your breathing, and directing the mind to the present moment without drifting its attention to the past or future. Mindfulness meditation can work wonders for people trying to cope with depression, anxiety, or chronic pain.

6. Exercise

Did you know people who exercise daily are less likely to experience stress and anxiety than those who don't? This is because any sort of physical exercise reduces the level of the stress hormone, cortisol, in your body. It releases chemicals, known as endorphins, which enhances mood and act as a natural pain reliever. Moreover, exercising helps to improve the quality of sleep that is often affected negatively due to anxiety and stress. Pick an exercise routine or activity that appeals to you. Dancing, cycling, jogging, and walking are some of the best de-stress activities to choose from.

7. Yoga

Yoga is a body-mind practice, which combines controlled breathing, physical poses, and relaxation or meditation. It brings about mental and physical disciplines that can help you achieve peacefulness of mind and body. This, in turn, helps you relax and manage stress and anxiety.

Experts suggest certain yoga postures are particularly beneficial for reducing stress. The most common and easy-to-practice poses are

Sukhasana/ Easy Pose with Forward Bend

Uttanasana/ Standing Forward Bend

Prasarita Padottanasana

Sasangasana/ Rabbit Pose

Vajrasana (Thunderbolt Pose) with Gadurasana (Eagle Pose)

Side Stretch

Halasana/ Plow Pose

Savasana/ Corpse Pose

Generalized anxiety disorder and yoga

Studies have reaffirmed that yoga has a lasting effect on symptom relief in depressed patients. A psychiatrist at Boston University School of Medicine, based on previous studies showing that yoga increases the amount of the neurotransmitter gamma-aminobutyric acid (GABA), as well as antidepressants and anxiolytics. Details of a study conducted by Chris Streeter and colleagues were published in the November Issue of the Journal of Psychiatric Practice.

The study was conducted over a 12-week period in 30 depressed adult patients. All but two of the subjects were taking antidepressants. Streeter and colleagues take half of the subjects in 90-minute yoga classes three times a week + 30-minute yoga "homework" four times a week in the "high-dose" yoga group, with the remaining half of 90 one-minute yoga classes twice a week + 30 minutes of yoga homework assigned to a "low-dose" yoga group doing three times a week at home. Total time spent doing yoga during the study was 123 hours in the high-dose yoga group and 87 hours in the low-dose yoga group. According to Streeter et al, The purpose of this study was to find the appropriate "dose" (frequency and time) of yoga, so we did not set up a control group without yoga.

As a result, in both the "high-dose" and "low-dose" yoga groups, feelings became more positive and calm, and symptoms such as physical fatigue, depression, and anxiety were alleviated. It was also shown that these effects increased as the amount of time spent on yoga and breathing exercises increased. However, the difference observed between the two groups was not statistically significant.

Streeter and colleagues suspect that this may be due to the small number of participants in the study and stated that a larger study needs to be conducted to verify the results. It should also be noted that this study did not demonstrate a causal relationship.

Inoltre, l'effetto dello yoga è durato 4 giorni, ma non è stato osservato alcun effetto dopo 8 giorni. Ciò suggerisce che "potrebbe essere necessario praticare regolarmente yoga per controllare i sintomi della depressione", ha detto Streeter. "Se lo yoga migliora i sintomi della depressione, potrebbe essere meglio prendere lo yoga una volta ogni due settimane".

In questo studio, è stato esaminato l'effetto dello yoga Iyengar sui sintomi depressivi. Iyengar yoga è un tipo di yoga che enfatizza il mantenimento di varie pose nella postura corretta per un tempo relativamente lungo e il controllo della respirazione. Ma Streeter ha detto: "Altri tipi di yoga daranno risultati simili".

Studi precedenti hanno dimostrato che l'esercizio fisico è efficace nel ridurre i sintomi nei pazienti depressi, ma Streeter ha detto: "Tra gli esercizi, lo yoga può avere un effetto positivo sui pazienti depressi". Mostra il punto di vista. "Lo yoga ha un elemento mentale unico che lo distingue dagli altri esercizi", ha detto Gregory Brown, psichiatra e istruttore di yoga presso il Green Psychiatry Center. La struttura di Brown utilizza lo yoga come "integratore" oltre ai tradizionali trattamenti per la depressione, i disturbi d'ansia e i disturbi da stress post-traumatico (PTSD).

"Le persone sospettose tendono a concentrarsi sui limiti della ricerca, ma sono più interessato a come possiamo espandere questo tipo di ricerca", ha detto Brown in risposta al rapporto di Streeter. "Lo yoga può essere un'opzione interessante per i pazienti che vogliono ridurre ulteriormente i sintomi della depressione o che vogliono evitare i farmaci", ha detto. Ho grandi aspettative.

Takeaway

Stress, if not managed effectively, can take a toll on your daily life, and make you susceptible to a host of health problems. Learning the basics of different types of relaxation techniques is quite easy. However, it takes regular practice to truly harness the power of relieving stress.

How Exercise Can Reduce Anxiety

You probably already know that if you exercise regularly a good workout can help you feel less stressed and better able to cope with problems. But can exercise help people with significant anxiety? Studies have found that physical activity can not only reduce anxiety symptoms, it can improve quality of life.

Just how exercise helps anxiety isn't known, but researchers believe that a combination of factors most likely come into play. For one thing, endorphins, the body's feel good chemical, is increased every time we exercise. Exercise probably helps ease anxiety by releasing other feel-good brain chemicals that effect neurotransmitters. Is also increases body temperature, which tends to induce a sense of calm. The act of exercising can build self-esteem and confidence and can provide social interaction when done with others.

Researchers examining exercise and anxiety have recommended that clinicians strongly encourage people with anxiety to exercise regularly in addition to adhering to proven treatment programs. Besides boosting mood, regular exercise offers a host of other benefits, such as reducing hypertension, reducing the risk of both heart disease and cancer, and preventing diabetes.

Therapists who do anxiety counseling routinely access the activity levels of their clients with anxiety. Almost any type of exercise can help to alleviate anxiety, but research has indicated that some types may be more antiolytic than others.

Yoga, in particular, has been shown to reduce anxiety and stress in a wide variety of contexts. After the 2004 Andaman tsunami, a study looked at the effect of yoga in reducing fear, anxiety, sadness and sleep problems in 47 of the survivors. Measurements of heart rate, breath, and skin resistance were used as markers. A significant decrease was detected in all markers, concluding that yoga was a useful intervention for anxiety and stress management particularly when combined with therapy.

In other research, yoga has reduced the signs of anxiety in people with eating disorders, cardiovascular disease, irritable bowel syndrome, and cancer. Moreover, yoga can be done by any age group and can be easily adapted for people with disabilities.

If someone has an anxiety disorder, typical treatment protocols include medication and psychotherapy. Often therapy includes the therapist attempting to get the client more motivated in terms of self-care including exercise, diet, and sleep.

The word "exercise" may make you think of exhausting yourself, running laps around the block. But exercise includes a wide range of activities that boost your activity level to help you feel better. Any activity that gets your heart pumping, such as running and lifting weights, is good but even brisk walking is helpful. Many people report that gardening, washing the car and other less intense activities are also helpful in reducing anxiety. Basically any form of exercise that gets the body moving stands a good chance of alleviating anxiety and calming the mind.

Anxiety Worksheets

1. Help for Anxious People: Literacy and Life Skills by Angela Ramsay

This anxiety workbook from Angela Ramsay is an excellent resource for improving your understanding of anxiety, learning how to get help for it, and what you can do on an individual level to address the challenges that constant anxiety can bring.

Ramsay covers the basics of anxiety, discusses some general differences between men and women when it comes to anxiety, and even reviews anxiety in children.

In the first chapter, "Understanding Anxiety," Ramsay (2003) aims to help the reader:

Define anxiety.

Describe when anxiety is normal.

Give an example of the "Assess-Plan-Act" Technique

Anxiety is defined in this workbook as "a feeling of fear, dread, or uneasiness" that is naturally occurring and even adaptive in the right doses. Ramsay notes that many situations will spark episodes of anxiety, including:

Exams or tests;

Strict deadlines;

Job interviews;

Waiting for a baby to be born;

Waiting to hear how a loved one fared after an accident or illness;

Traffic accidents;

Getting bad news;

or losing your job.

Help for Anxious People: Literacy and Life Skills by Angela Ramsay

These are all normal scenarios where the majority of people might get a little bit anxious. This anxiety is not necessarily a "bad" thing—it just is. It might even encourage you to be more aware of your environment, alert to danger, protective of yourself, and cautious.

In certain situations, anxiety injects a life-saving boost of adrenaline!

Some people do not experience anxiety every now and then; instead, it is a constant or heightened level of anxiety that causes incessant rumination and fear.

These people may be suffering from a condition such as:

Phobias;

Panic attacks;

Post-traumatic stress disorder;

Generalized Anxiety Disorder (GAD);

Obsessive-Compulsive Disorder (OCD);

and Depression.

As you make your way through the workbook, you will learn much more about anxiety, obsessions, and compulsions. For example, Ramsay notes that women are generally more anxious than men, in part due to hormonal differences (and sometimes influenced by the hormonal ups and downs of the menstrual cycle).

Meanwhile, men are less likely to feel anxiety (or at least less likely to admit to feeling anxiety) and tend to feel anxious about things like their health. Social pressures and expectations on gender performance may be part of these perceived differences.

Ramsay also includes helpful exercises and activities for processing your anxiety, with immediately impactful activities to build your skills to battle anxiety over time.

One immediately impactful activity encouraged by Ramsay is the Relaxation Exercise 2, on page 11 of the PDF. This exercise is described below.

Relaxation Exercise

Before you begin this exercise, make sure that you will not be disturbed. We have broken it down into 15 simple steps that are easy to follow:

1. Take a comfortable seat, close your eyes, and remind yourself that you have nothing to do right now. There may be things that need to get done later, but for now, you have no problems that need immediate solving.

2. Take a deep breath and slowly exhale. Repeat the words "I am peace" to yourself a few times.

3. Don't try to relax, just permit yourself to relax. Let go and allow yourself to simply be.

4. Think of your body as a part of the earth itself, like a mountain—still and quiet.

5. Sink deeper into the surface beneath you, and let your eyes gently roll upwards behind your closed lids. Imagine that you can see the world, or just sense the words "I am peace" written there on the back of your mind.

6. As you see or sense these words, "I am peace," you may feel a gentle fluttering of your eyelids; this means they are becoming relaxed. Feel the warm, moist feeling behind your eyelids and melt into it. Let relaxation flow into and through your body.

7. No matter how relaxed you become, you may notice that you can always become more relaxed. Use imagery such as visualizing yourself strolling through a peaceful garden or down a quiet, sandy beach, to slip deeper into your relaxation.

8. You can feel yourself becoming more and more relaxed.... Just letting go... Becoming more and more comfortable as time goes on.

9. Allow all of your physical tension to leave your body and leave all unnecessary or unhelpful thoughts at the metaphorical door.

10. When you are feeling completely peaceful, imagine that you're standing beneath a gentle waterfall. The warm, crystal clear water is falling softly on your head and flowing down your body to your toes. Feel the sensation of being cleansed from head to toe.

11. If you find unnecessary thoughts or questions entering your mind, imagine they are like words written in the sand—with your next exhale, see the words being wiped away by a sweeping wave, leaving the only smooth sand and little bubbles glistening in the sun.

12. In your head, travel to a private and peaceful place, somewhere in the present, past, or future. It may be an island, a beach, a forest, or any other place where you feel calm, safe, and happy. Stay here for as long as you like, soaking up the calm feelings and gathering any peace.

13. When you are ready to come back to your day, pause in your happy place. Gradually allow yourself to awake from your calm and peaceful place, a little bit at a time.

14. You are coming up slowly as if you're waking up from a good night's sleep or a refreshing nap. You feel alert, rested, and ready to tackle whatever is ahead of you.

15. While you are now fully awake, make sure to take a little bit of that peace you harnessed. Hang on to a bit of that relaxation and carry it with you throughout your day.

Anxiety Inventory

Another helpful tool in this book is the Burns Anxiety Inventory, which can help the reader determine how big of a problem their anxiety is, and in which areas they are most vulnerable to it (Burns, 1999).

To complete the inventory, the reader will rate 33 statements on how often they have felt that way or identified with that statement in the past week on a scale from 0 (not at all) to 3 (a lot). There are three categories of symptoms, Anxious Feelings, Anxious Thoughts, and Physical Symptoms, with several items each. For example, one item from Anxious Feelings is "Feeling that things around you are strange, unreal, or foggy."

An example item of Anxious Thoughts reads "Concerns about looking foolish or inadequate in front of others." Finally, one of the Physical Symptoms items is "Butterflies or discomfort in the stomach."

The reader should rate each statement and add up the total score for all 33 symptoms and use the following rubric to determine whether their anxiety lies along the spectrum from "none at all" to "constant anxiety":

0 – 4: Minimal or no anxiety

5 – 10: Borderline anxiety

11 – 20: Mild anxiety

21 – 30: Moderate anxiety

31 – 50: Severe anxiety

51 – 99: Extreme anxiety or panic

This will give readers an idea of the extent to which their anxiety is a significant problem in their day-to-day life. They can also track their progress in reducing their anxiety by taking it each week, or more often if they feel they are improving rapidly, to compare scores over time.

This handbook (as well as its companion book) is a bestseller and has helped thousands of people manage their anxiety and other emotional problems.

How to Practice Mindfulness Meditation

This workbook can be helpful whether the reader is working through it alone or as a complement to therapy or counseling with a mental health professional. Its goal is to help the reader build the necessary skills for squashing overly-anxious thoughts and putting yourself back in control of your thoughts and feelings.

Mindfulness meditation is a simple tool you can use to keep your attention focused on the present, without judgment.

Sitting meditation simply involves relaxing into an upright position and using the breath as the focus of attention.

It then guides you step by step through an uninterrupted, mindfulness meditation exercise that should ideally be practiced for around 10-15 minutes daily if you'd like to make it a habit.

Some helpful tips include:

Keeping a straight, upright, but not stiff back

Making sure that your knees are lower than your hips, to self-support your spine with a gently curving lower back

If in a chair, place the soles of your feet on the ground. If on the floor, cross your legs.

Let your arms fall naturally to your sides, with your palms resting on your thighs.

If your pose becomes too uncomfortable, feel free to take a break or adjust.

Because the sensations of breathing are always present, they are useful as a tool to help you focus on the present moment. Whenever you become distracted during meditation, turn your focus back to breathing.

Notice the sensation of air as it passes through your nose or mouth, the rise and fall of your belly, and the feeling of air being exhaled, back into the world. Notice the sounds that accompany each inhalation and exhalation.

Many people feel as though meditation is something that needs to be performed "well," which can cause unnecessary stress. For that reason, you'll also find plenty of helpful advice in this resource on how to deal with wandering thoughts—which are normal.

Instead of struggling against your thoughts, simply notice them without judgment. Acknowledge that your mind has wandered, and then return your attention to breathing. Expect to repeat this process again and again.

This exercise has so much potential to help with anxiety because mindfulness meditation is a powerful tool. Those who practice it regularly boost awareness and improve the ability to remain objective and neutral to what is happening around them, even when caught in a hurricane of emotions, thoughts, and actions.

Exercise to solve your worries

Many people have wondered, "How can I get in shape faster?" But when you actually start a workout, it's very easy to make excuses that you don't have to (especially during the Christmas season).

At the beginning of a workout, endurance is not the best. It takes some getting used to. So, I tried to summarize how to get me more exercise without feeling like I'm doing the hardest thing in the world.

10 exercises to easily train your body

Also continues 1:10 times

Try push-ups only 10 times. They don't have to be 10 times a day in a row. It's better than not doing them and after a while you'll feel comfortable doing 10 times and can increase the number at your own pace.

2: Get up at least once every hour

Probabilmente hai letto un articolo che sporgendoti in avanti sulla tastiera, non uscire a pranzo troppo occupato e stare seduto tutto il giorno fa male.

Sforzati di alzarti consapevolmente una volta ogni ora. Puoi semplicemente andare in bagno, preparare il tè o parlare con il posto di un collega. Ancora meglio, acquista un Apple Watch. Se il sensore rileva che non è stato avviato, ti avviserà 10 minuti prima di ogni ora.

3: Cammina per almeno 20 minuti al giorno

Che sia freddo o meno in pieno inverno, camminare per 20 minuti al giorno migliorerà la tua salute. È facile da incorporare nel tuo programma quotidiano e non devi respirare.

Walk 20 minutes a day and see how this alone can make the difference between your health and well-being.

4: Train at home where you can relax

You don't have to leave the house to get a solid workout, and you don't even have to leave your couch. There are many practical exercises and home workouts you can do in your living room without going to the gym. Try triceps dips (triceps brachial flexion), lunges (muscle training with your own weights), abdominal crunches, etc. In a relaxed environment at home.

5: Use the TABATA formation

If you only have 5 minutes , download the TABATA Timer app for a super fast workout. A high-intensity workout that guides you through 20 seconds of exercise and 10 seconds of rest as a set, and is effective for both fitness and weight loss.

If you run for 20 seconds, walk for 10 seconds or if you jump for 20 seconds, lie down for 10 seconds. You can do burpees, climbers and planks, and Tabata training can quickly increase your metabolism and heart rate, so you'll see the benefits right away.

6: Turn off the device

Exercise is not the only thing. Daily living affects your health and wellness. Getting enough sleep is essential for fitness, but if you're distracted by a variety of devices every day, it's pointless.

So turn off all devices at least an hour before you fall asleep. Then you should be able to get better rest.

7: Don't worry about how long you'll continue your workout

The quality of your workout doesn't matter how long you've been doing it. Any exercise is great and the most important thing to start with is physical activity.

Don't try to climb the mountain before you can walk. It doesn't matter if you don't do it for an hour or if you can't run as much as you think. It is important that you are getting some type of exercise.

8: Play only one song of music

Tell yourself to only perform one song for the moment, rather than being overly ambitious and having trouble practicing and despising yourself. If you pick one good song, you won't even notice that three and a half minutes have passed.

9. Have sex in bed

Let's see the reality. Some exercise is fun and sex is one of them. A study conducted by scientists at the University of Quebec in Canada found that sexual activity was just as effective as medium-intensity exercise in consuming energy.

It is said that a woman burns about 90 calories in one sex, which is about half of 30 minutes of jogging.

10: Exercise during the advertisement

Watching TV is a relaxing pastime for everyone. So why not combine it with exercise and do a mini-workout only during the commercials? If you do a 5-minute circuit like lunges, burpees, jogs, skips, squats during the commercial, you can lie down on the couch as a reward.

The effect of sport on the brain

Exercise activates our brain and calms us down at the same time. This allows us to be more active and calmer. A study reveals the difference between the brains of exercising and under-exercising mice. Researchers at Princeton University focused on this seemingly contradictory problem and conducted experiments on mice. One mouse was given free access to the exercise wheels, while the other was left stationary. And a special substance made them colorful as new cells sprang up in their brains.

After 6 weeks, the mice's stress levels were measured. The exercise mice were more exploratory and tended to spend time outdoors if possible. In contrast, the under-exercised mice showed more fear and anxiety as they approached places they had never been. In addition, the former had many new neurons and was very active, while the latter was the opposite.

At the same time, the brains of the physically active mice had a large number of neurons that could release the neurotransmitter GABA (Gamma Amino Butyric Acid). This is a neurotransmitter that suppresses brain activity and calms excessive arousal. These neurons were concentrated in the hippocampal region involved in emotion. What does it do?

The researchers put the mice in cold water for 5 minutes. This is an uncomfortable and stressful situation. Again, the reaction of the mice's brains was divided by "whether they were exercising or not." Although all mice showed significant brain arousal, the first group of mice were quickly able to suppress fear and anxiety. The effects of the stress did not last long. Their brains activated a large number of "sedative" neurons capable of releasing GABA, which could quickly calm excessive anxiety. The missing mice, on the other hand, were long fascinated by the anxiety caused by cold water baths.

"Not only are the neurons observed to be more active and have more synapses, but more neurons are" reaction inhibitors "that restrain brain processes when they are overexcited."

This allows the training mice to be more active and more relaxed at the same time.

Importantly, the beneficial effects of the sport last a long time. "I tried stopping the exercise wheels 24 hours before the cold water bath. The mice in the exercise group couldn't do any new exercise to get the effect, but they already did. It turned out that the exercise was sufficient . The difference in their response was solely due to the structure of the brain, which was already different from the other mice."

Obviously, human and mouse brains are not the same, but other studies in humans have shown that exercise relieves stress (although it is unclear whether the various neurons are